Let's Visit the Post Office

Marianne Johnston

The Rosen Publishing Group's
PowerKids Press™
New York

Published in 2000 by The Rosen Publishing Group, Inc.
29 East 21st Street, New York, NY 10010

First Edition

Book design: Danielle Primiceri

Photo Credits: pp. 4, 11, 12 © Bonnie Rothstein-Brewer; pp. 6, 8 © CORBIS/Bettmann; p. 7 © Culver Pictures; p. 15 © Jeffrey Sylvester/FPG International; pp. 16, 20 © R. Rathe/FPG International; p. 17 © Telegraph Colour Library/FPG International; p. 19 © Bill Losh/FPG International.

Johnston, Marianne.
    Let's visit the post office / by Marianne Johnston.
        p.   cm. — (Our community)
    Includes index.
    Summary: A simple introduction to the functions of the United States postal service, how the work is accomplished, and the impact it has on the community.
    ISBN 0-8239-5433-1 (lib. bdg. : alk. paper)
    1. Postal service—United States—Juvenile literature. [1. Postal service.] I. Title. II. Series: Johnston, Marianne. Our community.
HE6371.J64   1999
383'.4973—dc21   98-18010
                                                   CIP

Manufactured in the United States of America

Contents

What Does the Post Office Do?

Isn't it fun to get birthday cards in the mail? How about getting a letter from a friend or family member? Keeping in touch with people is a big part of belonging to a **community**. Without the post office, it would be very hard to get letters to your friends and neighbors. It would be even harder to get letters to people who lived outside of your own neighborhood.

The people who work at the post office are proud to help the people in their communities. They make sure the mail gets delivered as quickly and as safely as possible.

The post office helps people in the commmunity keep in touch.

The History of Mail

In the 1600s, America didn't have post offices like the ones we have today. In Boston, a restaurant owned by a man named Richard Fairbanks became the first official post office in the Colonies. Travelers or salespeople passing through a town on the way to Boston would bring mail and messages with them. Once they got there, they would drop the mail off at Richard Fairbanks' restaurant.

FUN FACTS

In 1775, Ben Franklin was named the first Postmaster General by the Continental Congress.

A lot of the mail that was sent in the 1600s was going to England. ▶

POST OFFICE

The Pony Express

In 1860, the famous **Pony Express** began. Instead of traveling by wagon or by ship, mail would be sent from towns in the East to St. Joseph, Missouri by train. Mail carriers would pick it up at the post office in St. Joseph and ride on horseback to deliver it out West. The Pony Express **mail carrier** would deliver his mail to Sacramento, California. From there, postal workers delivered the mail to different towns in the West.

FUN FACTS

In 1863, a letter cost 3 cents to mail anywhere in the country. Today it costs 33 cents!

◀ *Pony Express mail carriers had to ride for about 10 days straight.*

9

The Post Office Today

The **postal service** has grown into a huge system that can deliver mail to just about every corner of our country, and the world. To send a letter, you need to buy a stamp from the post office. This tells the post office workers that you have paid to have your letter delivered. Once the stamp is on the envelope, you can place your letter in a blue mailbox on the street corner to be picked up.

FUN FACTS

Mules deliver 2,000 pounds of mail a week to the people who live in the Grand Canyon.

Stamps show that you have paid to have your letter delivered. ▶

The Post Office Window

When you walk into the post office, you will usually see a person sitting behind a counter. This person is the window clerk, and the counter is the post office window. The clerk helps all the people from your community who come into the post office. He or she sells stamps to customers. The window clerk also helps people send their packages. First, the window clerk sees how much the package weighs. Next, he or she figures out how much sending that package will cost based on its weight.

◄ *The window clerk will give you a sticker showing that you've paid to mail your package.*

13

In the Back of the Post Office

Once your mail goes through the hands of the window clerk, it gets taken to the back of the post office. A **mail clerk** divides the mail up into local and out-of-town mail. Local mail is going somewhere in that town. Out-of-town mail is going to other towns or cities.

The local mail stays in the post office. The out-of-town mail gets put into large, gray or white canvas bags and loaded onto a mail truck by a **mail handler**. The trucks head for a **distribution center**. Mail from several post offices gets delivered to this huge building.

This postal worker is sending letters through a sorting machine. ▶

At the Distribution Center

At the distribution center, the mail from many post offices is dumped onto big conveyor belts that take the letters to sorting machines. Short railings along the sides of the belts keep the letters from falling off. Thousands of letters are carried on these belts that criss-cross each floor of the building. The letters then zip through the sorting machines. The machines read the addresses and sort the letters for different communities.

Tons of mail goes through the distribution center each day.

FUN FACTS

One distribution center can have 5 miles of conveyor belts.

17

Sorting the Mail for the Carriers

The mail carrier is the person who delivers the mail to homes and businesses in your community. Each mail carrier has a specific **route** that he must deliver mail to.

When he gets to work at about 6:00 A.M., the mail carrier must sort all of the mail for his route by address. The carrier bundles up the sorted mail and loads it into the mail truck. Now he is ready to deliver the mail.

18

The mail carrier is an important person in the community. ▶

Technology at the Post Office

Your community post office has to deal with a lot of mail every day. Machines help the people at the post office get their work done.

Sorting machines can sort nine letters per second. Before machines came along, people had to sort the mail by hand. At the distribution centers, computer screens show a map of all the belts in the building. If one stops working, a light on the map will blink, showing where the problem is.

Technology has made sorting the mail a lot faster and easier.

21

How Grandma Got Her Letter

Joan wrote a letter to her grandmother. She stamped the envelope and put it in the blue mailbox on the street corner. Betty, the neighborhood mail carrier, picked up the letter and took it to the post office. Joan's letter was sent to the distribution center and through the sorting machines. Mail clerks there made sure it got on the mail truck that was headed to Grandma's town.

Web Sites:

For more information on the post office, check out this Web site: http://www.usps.gov

Glossary

community (kuh-MYOO-nih-tee) A group of people who have something in common, such as a special interest or the area where they live.

distribution center (dis-trih-BYOO-shun SEN-ter) A big building where mail from post offices and mail boxes come in to be sorted.

mail carrier (MAYL KAR-ee-ur) The postal worker who delivers your mail to your mailbox.

mail clerk (MAYL KLERK) The person who works behind the scenes at the post office sorting mail.

mail handler (MAYL HAND-ler) The person who works behind the scenes at the post office loading mail onto the trucks and sorting heavy packages.

Pony Express (POH-nee ecks-PRES) The mail delivery system used from 1860-1862 to deliver mail by horse to the western part of the United States.

postal service (POH-stul SUR-vis) The entire system of post offices and mail handling in the United States.

route (ROOT) The fixed course a mail carrier takes to deliver the mail.

Index